The Moment's Equation

Poems by

Vern Rutsala

The Ashland Poetry Press
Ashland University
Ashland, Ohio 44805

Acknowledgement is made to editors of the following publications in which these poems, sometimes in somewhat different form, originally appeared.

Agni: Portland Hosts the Second Coming, What the World Does
Aisling: On Transcendence
The American Poetry Review: The Boneyard
The American Scholar: Shame
The Atlantic: The Windowsill Over the Sink, Traffic Watch
Calapooya Collage: Billie Holiday, Bleached Grass
The Chariton Review: Blake in Idaho
College English: Home Remedies
Colorado Review: Carpentry
Crab Orchard Review: Fifteen
Crazyhorse: Cards from My Aunt, Field Burning
Fine Madness: August Memories
The Georgia Review: Specter
The Gettysburg Review: What's Out There Now
The Kenyon Review: Raisins
The Massachusetts Review: The Goodbye Series
Mud Creek Review: Families Returning
Nebraska Review: Sunday Morning Walk
Open Spaces: Cannon Beach Meditation
The Ohio Poetry Review: Real Things, Numbers Game
Poetry: WWII
Poetry NOW: Tom Pete
Portland: The Old Place
Portland Review: Enough
Rain City Review: Industrial Relations
Seattle Review: The Forgetful House
The Sewanee Review: Fret, Change, Romance, Pastoral
Southern Poetry Review: Reunion on the Weekend of the Fourth, Ancestors Office Hours and Drought
Sycamore Review: The Moment's Equation
The Talking of Hands (New Rivers Press): Geography
Tar River Poetry: Run Sheep Run
Three Rivers Poetry Journal: American Names
West Branch: Slivers

"Billie Holiday" and "Bleached Grass" were awarded the Carolyn
Kizer Poetry Prize. The author wants to thank the Oregon Arts
Commission for a Masters Fellowship which provided time for the
completion of a number of these poems. "On Transcendence" and
"Enough" appeared in *The Mystery of Lost Shoes*, a chapbook pub-
lished by Lynx House Press.

Printed in the United States of America

ISBN: 0-912592-54-0

Library of Congress Catalog Card Number: 2004110182

Cover drawing: *Tools & Runes*, by Vern Rutsala

Contents

III.

To Joan

I

Traffic Watch

As always it is late, the freeways
        trickling with late drivers
kept in town by the impossible

debt, the mortgage that falls due
        every second, kept late by fears
of home—house and family

ready to swallow them one button
        at a time, paycheck
by paycheck. Looking down I follow

their quiet lights nosing along
        like insects as they look for
the one driveway that will take

them in. I see them pull into
        garages with great stealth
in order to keep the tools asleep—

mowers slumped in winter hibernation,
        ladders in attitudes of prayer.
There is the click of the door

and the aching pause as the road
        plucks at their sleeves
to call them back—one more drink,

that smile across the room, the safe
        limbo of the dark bar.
But it is too late and they reenter

the dreaded door, trying to remember
        the story they should tell of lateness
and despair, the one they never tell

and never will, or how the worm
      of hopelessness lies coiled
in the very heart of hope.

Shame

This is the shame of the woman whose hand hides
her smile because her teeth are bad, not the grand
self-hate that leads some to razors or pills
or swan dives off beautiful bridges however
tragic that is. This is the shame of being yourself,
of being ashamed of where you live and what
your father's paycheck lets you eat and wear.
This is the shame of the fat and the old,
the unbearable blush of acne, the shame of having
no lunch money and pretending you're not hungry.
This is the shame of concealed sickness—diseases
too expensive to afford that offer only their cold
one-way tickets out. This is the shame of being ashamed,
the self-disgust of the cheap wine-drunk, the lassitude
that makes junk accumulate, the shame that tells
you there is another way to live but you are
too dumb to find it. This is the real shame, the damned
shame, the crying shame, the shame that's criminal,
the shame of knowing words like 'glory' are not
in your vocabulary though they litter the Bibles
you're still paying for. This is the shame of not
knowing how to read and pretending you do. This is
the shame that makes you afraid to leave your house,
the shame of food stamps at the supermarket when
the clerk shows impatience as you fumble with the change.
This is the shame of dirty underwear, the shame
of pretending your father works in an office
as God intended all men to do. This is the shame
of asking friends to let you off in front of the one
nice house in the neighborhood and waiting
in shadows until they drive away before walking
to the gloom of your house. This is the shame
at the end of the mania for owning things, the shame
of no heat in winter, the shame of eating cat food,
the unholy shame of dreaming of a new house and car
and the shame of knowing how cheap such dreams are.

American Names

Tonight I think of those relatives
who changed their names, cut loose
from the stigma of all those Finnish
vowels, and lost in phone books under

the protective coloring of Anglo-Saxon
like Jimmy Gatz fading into Gatsby
with all those beautiful shirts.
One uncle in fact was like old Jay,

calling himself Russell and making
a big splash with frozen foods in Seattle.
We visited him there a few times—
he always met us in restaurants with

menus too big to hold comfortably
and never took us home to meet his wife.
We knew we embarrassed him but struggled
through the menu, admiring the fancy

cut of his suit and the big tips he gave.
Driving home we guessed he had invented
a past we could be no part of which seemed
fair enough but after the third visit

we never went again—the restaurants
were fancy but the food wasn't much
and those menus always made us nervous.
Years later we heard that Daisy divorced

him anyway after his sharp partners
dumped him, and he died of a business man's
disease at fifty-three with only the shirt
on his back and a second-hand Cadillac

they auctioned off to pay the funeral bill.

The Goodbye Series

That was the summer you drew the goodbye
        series and now those drawings are lost.
I remember huge hands waving from airplanes

and trains, long arms with sausage fingers
        waving from porches and doors, ballooning
from car windows. Everyone was saying goodbye

like Plastic Man, everyone was going
        somewhere, getting the hell out, you said,
before the fuse that always got Wile E. Coyote

burned all the way down. You drew those pictures
        waving to young men heading for Toronto
and Vancouver, lighting out for Winnipeg

and Montreal. But those ham hands waved to more
        than those men. They fluttered goodbye
to everything as it had been, as it would never

be again. Get a passport, you said, just in case.
        Goodbye was in the air, evenings cried farewell,
a haze of valediction over us all, and "Waist Deep

in the Big Muddy" was the song we sang as summer
        died within us. We knew some who drove fast
to the center of madness, waving goodbye, goodbye,

confusing Teddy Bears and bombs, wanting their
        childhoods to come back and sing them to sleep
one more time. Others heard secret messages

in radio songs or saw signs on album covers, saying
        goodbye to words and you drew the goodbye
series as the civil rights of hair became a passion.

I don't know where those drawings are or where
        you've gone but I see them clearly—
stovepipe arms and hands like blimps with fingers.

We sank deeper and deeper into the Big Muddy
        waving goodbye to history, goodbye to love,
our hands growing huge as we waved and waved.

What the World Does

What about Aunt Jenny's piece of the American dream?
She spent thirty years of eyesight sewing
for White Stag. Doesn't that count for something?
She gave me factory-second ski jackets
every Christmas though I never skied—it was
a sport for rich kids anyway. The flaws were
hard to find—like almost perfect forgeries.
She lived in the same greasy apartment all
those years—the same one-armed chair I read
comics in at ten still there when she died.
Didn't America have at least one chair to spare?
Or an arm at least? It was the emblem of what
the world taught her—put up with things,
keep your nose clean or the Depression might
loom over you again, snapping your job right out
of your hands. This is what the world does.
There was that wedding gift she sent, packed in
a Jim Beam box—such promise!—but rattling and too
heavy for booze. Anger tickled my throat—the old
apartment, that chair, factory seconds, her
lost eyesight—and I tore the carton open.
Out spewed a welter of flatware looking like
the poor threw it out fifty years ago, looking
like it would dissolve in soup or turn your whole
life the color of cheap tin. With a rage of sadness
I threw that pathos across the floor—that cheap
clatter the leaden music of her airless rooms,
the greasy walls, the slumping chair, the lessons
the world drummed into her over and over,
telling her there was no other way to live,
a way she now tried to pass on as if enlisting us
in some cramped conspiracy against life.
This is what the world does. Tonight I unwrap
that package again, remembering how its contents
lurched and rattled, and the old rage returns,
a rage against the helplessness that made

9

her pour her eyes down a billion needle holes
making clothes for the rich, working for skinflint
bosses whose dyspeptic smiles she courted,
living year after year in that gloom,
and thinking such hopeless knives and forks,
too grim to even be second-hand, could be the wedding
gift to start us on our quest for the American
dream she believed in with all her heart.

Change

In agate type the sports page lists
Transactions—so and so traded,
someone put on injured reserve,
another waived out of the league.
Such lists uncover the sadness
of change and separation—our
own lives dwindling into fine print
with the aging bonus baby
sent down to double A, his great
hopes and ours a faint blur
on page four. We think of such players
gone to a kind of limbo, bat
and ball denied them, carrying
only their scuffed shoes down some road
of sore arms and bad knees. We eke
out our days among the injured
reserves—like us they may be fit
some day—but feel ourselves sliding
toward the saddest of all,
that invisible leavening of all
trades during the hot stove league,
players who don't even have names,
the players to be named later.

The Windowsill Over the Sink

You're back from a long trip
and promise yourself
that it will never be cluttered
again. Yet you see it grow
its inhabitants almost by stealth:
A horse chestnut, votive candles,
paper clips and safety pins,
the accumulation gathering around
the aspirin bottle. Then the cup
with the broken handle, the bird's nest
found on a walk, pinecones,
matchbooks, coupons offering
ten cents off on a Mercedes.
The old life is reentered this way
and begins to crowd around you
with its clutter showing again that
you can keep everything but promises.

Home Remedies

These days we come home
needing repair, carrying

the fly-buzz of confusion,
arms full of rotten apples,

our hearts pleated with aches,
our eyes and fingers

crossed with a need
for cure. A need

for necklaces of garlic,
for bear and goose grease,

chicken soup, poultice
and magic chant to clear

the liars from our lives
like phlegm. But we settle in

and settle for a drink,
slow talk, broken bread,

and love's sweet
stopgap repairs.

Raisins

Our pettiness is endless.
Like the ancient raisin I

noticed ground into the soft
wood on the landing, and I

remembered telling you
to stop scattering raisins all

over the house. That was years
ago when you listened to me

or at least pretended to—
I remember scraping up

a lot of raisins though
but I don't know why I cared.

At times the other night it seemed
we were both doomed to teach

ourselves other languages,
different ones, so we would

never have to speak again,
or live so far apart

no operator could ever
connect us. You are sleeping

now, your bags packed, and all
the words left unsaid come down

to this raisin, more floor than
raisin now, that says so much

about the ancient pain of fathers
and children: Things that

mattered once no longer do.
Like that anger we shared

the other night as we've shared
this address for so long—that coal

of anger each of us blew on
to keep it burning.

The Forgetful House

By now it's forgotten
          everything on purpose—
                    dryrot amnesia
settled deep in its
          bones. Just driving by
                    you can tell—somehow
it's even lost its
          number, listing to one
                    side that way, changing
color. No room
          in such a place
                    would dare remember
them, not even a flimsy
          echo as they rinsed a cup
                    or drummed the hours
numb with their fingers.
          Now it's just a house
                    you can't count on,
a house dedicated
          to forgetting every sound.
                    This is why you don't
stop—you can see it in
          the windows like
                    dirty blackboards, the ragged
fingernails of the tired
          shingles and that
                    wanton screen door
hanging off-kilter.
          It even forgot
                    to keep the grass
from going crazy.
          You know it chewed
                    your labored letters
to pulp, milled all
          their last words
                    down to powder

out of careless
       spite, and deliberately
           misplaced their last
days, crammed
      in a drawer
          with old keys.

Specter

A helplessness no splint
can fix hobbles along our streets
tonight, the kind of sadness
Americans are so good at

ignoring, drawing their blinds.
But it's inside us
like a fever. Listen to our
laughter—it mumbles there,

a bass backing up the melody,
fathoms deep on the keyboard.
Its terrible limp tells the story
of conscripted dreams, barefoot

and anonymous. We try
to patch them up with bubble
gum and wisecracks. We try
the Palmer Method

and the Dewey Decimal System.
Nothing works. Alone, we whimper.
We want to back out on
the deal. All this winning

and losing. All this tragedy
spoiling our best jokes.
The house owns all the odds.
Winners are fakes anyway—

their money's only rented.
We grasp at the last straw
in our drink—surely Donald
Trump was happy, wasn't he?

The helplessness imbeds its
most famous charley horse in our
lives, our souls crammed in
our wallets, rubbing hard against

the filthy crippled bills.

Portland Hosts the Sceond Coming

At most we expect a touring company—
the original cast scheduled for Seattle—
which is exactly what we get.

Roadies and tarnished angels arrive first
by greyhound, looking sleepy in their
talkative T-shirts and miniskirts

more wrinkled than old winos' faces.
The angels are testy—their harps grew
icy and off-key in the belly of the bus.

They stand around hunching their shoulders
the way new arrivals always do, expecting
the worst. Most of them look like runaways—

in fact they begin working the streets
immediately. Local crazies hoot
but the angels snarl and say shove off

and solicit like mad, panhandling
the hell out of Old Town, landing
by radar at Third and Burnside.

They mumble about camels and needles
and people who own boutiques.
Then some giant steel band plays

loud and the sky goes crazy
with better fireworks than we expected.
Jim says, Not a bad show. I nod

and shade my eyes. Right then
the biggest log cabin in the world
builds itself again having instantly

forgotten the old overcoat of flames
that kept it too warm. The steel band
does a riff and the old Portland

Hotel shoulders through pavement,
knocking over high rises and pizza
joints and settles lightly

into its old place like it hadn't
gone anywhere. It's perfect, just like
its pictures. Demolished opera houses

and saloons resume their former
addresses with dignity and streetcars clang
down all the streets, jaunty and ten

cents a ride—a nickel for kids.
Hey, this ain't bad, Jim says. I nod.
All those condemned houses the jackleg

city fathers ate for lunch come back too
assuming their places on all fours,
lights on and cabbage cooking.

Lacy curtains flutter and a dog I
remember leans out his special window
and grins. Kids play hopscotch

where the Bank Tower stood using
broken bits of its vast windows
for markers. Like jack-in-the-boxes

old theaters are resurrected—
the Liberty still open all night,
the Blue Mouse, the Broadway

and lines form at their box offices
right away. Jim says, Smell that popcorn.
I nod, sniffing. And yes, the air

is sweet as the old lost skyline
that lets the hills just be hills.
Trees falsely accused of weird foreign

diseases sprout up and the city fathers
run like lemmings for their condos—
but their condos are zoned to smithereens.

The runaway angels and roadies dance
and sing with the winos and crazies,
drunker and crazier than they've

ever been. The steel band plays soft as rain
and everyone joins the revolution,
glad the original cast was too good for us.

The Old Place

I call in the ancient ghosts
of the livestock, soft muzzles
and snorts in the twilight,
heavy feet plodding in
as I quickly rebuild the barn
with its deep dark smell
and cloudy light. The animals
settle in their stalls
like heavy shadows.
And now I bring back my father
and his lost brothers,
all released from sepia's
dim restraint. Dazed, they
stretch and yawn, they've
slept so long. The smoky outline
of the house appears before them
as if through a fog
but the barn's firm dimensions
ease them back toward belief.
On the porch they yelp
and gasp, washing up
in the icy water, and find
themselves fully, flicking
rough towels at each other
and swearing, wondering where
the hell they've been so long.
The rest of the house is faint
and I run ahead of them
to make it real, driving
nails and painting in
the umber corners, adding
afterthoughts of age and wear
until they believe it easily
and walk in. The interior looms
up, my flashlight splashing
it back to life board by board.

They sit down at the long table
for their mother's heavy meal—
she hovers with their sister,
both seeming to skate in their
long dresses as they fill the plates
and glasses. Their father
keeps them all silent, presiding
as he always did and warns
the boys to come home early.
The brothers grin at each other
so he won't see, smacking their
lips for booze and fights and girls,
now ready for the Saturday
night dance at Finn Hall
where my father met my mother.

Run Sheep Run

There may be no road back,
those days going bright
and vague like overexposed
photos, then dimming
into some impenetrable ink
of the past. But we must try.
And somehow it drifts into being.
It was a wide field, above it
the log house with rough floors,
a blue checked cloth
on the long table, a stove
like a battleship, steam
from black iron pots of vast
and bubbling nourishment.
All of us, so many nephews
and nieces, so many sisters
and brothers, divided into
teams on the wide field.
And at the command we all
ran with ecstatic fear from
one side to the other—
Run Sheep Run!—through
twilight again and again until
the dark called us in
to eat from the huge iron pots
and then fall into sleep in fields
of swirling grass white as wool.

Cards from My Aunt

They come every year at Christmas,
written in a perfect Palmer
Method. We imagine her
still doing the exercises—rows

and rows of perfect O's
at the kitchen table. They come
every year but tell us too
little—we can't even read

between the lines. Among the usual
greetings there is always a phrase
out of the blue—"Haven't moved
yet" or "Sam is much improved."

Others have told us "The pollen
count was too high" and "It must
have been the full moon." We get
this piecemeal version of her life

once a year, a story all foreshadowing
or denouement, all punchline
without any buildup. In what way
has Sam improved? Was it

pollen or the moon that made
him sick? With lines dropped in
that way there is always
a sense of crisis just over

or about to happen but never
the thing itself, a kind of
off-stage drama we can never
fathom. All we can do

is crown her the heavyweight
champion of exasperation or queen
of the non sequitur. The last card
ended with, "You just can't

stop people from stealing."
Stealing what, Auntie? And how
is Sam now? Have you moved yet?
What is the pollen count on the moon?

Real Things

The real world hummed
far away—at home
grayness drained from
everything, leaking

into an air that
smelled fresh
if we had known
the difference.

We thought it
was only the aroma
of our insignificance.
Real things happened

in cities so far
away we knew
they had to be dreams.
Places where people

had names like
Claudette and Cary.
Real things happened
in skyscrapers

and ocean liners
and the neat
compartments of
silver trains we

never even heard
the whistles of.
We had our single
freight twice

a week loaded
with logs
and grayness.
Keeping things

small seemed
the best thing
we could do
so we whittled

a lot and managed
finally to turn
all our tall firs
into toothpicks.

The Boneyard

I touch only a sliver of a shank,
some pointed splintery hint
by way of legend but it is
enough and tonight the bones gather
and rattle, bleached white,
go hollow and light. The lightness
tells the story—the hollowness
like a dried gourd—of the warnings
the big wheels from Texas
wouldn't listen to. Winter, the locals
said, *Winter*. It should have been
enough but the cigars and Cadillacs
with steer horns on their hoods,
wouldn't hear. *Couldn't be nothing
like a blue norther,* they chuckled,
sneering at the local's weak sister
fears. *Nothing like the Panhandle
in December.* The locals nodded,
took the lease money but said
wait and see. The Texans trucked in
the fine longhorn herds in September,
the weather blue and bonny, winking
at the cheapness of wintering over
in such lush fields and sweet
water. They left the steers
to shift for themselves and drove
their empty truck herds home.
But October turned down the pilot
light, November brought the first
installment of snow, and December
drifted the map white. By January
the steers were beyond saving.
With the spring thaw only bones
and hides were found. Too polite
to say I told you so, the locals
did grin a little at how fast

the Texan's fat wallets went flat
but remembered and honored
the memory of the steers by calling
that range The Boneyard for years.

Romance

They hovered in the mist at evening,
whispering their way around
tables after supper, hints
and omens, some great coming
attraction lying in ambush
in the future. Warming up
it might simply be the shame
of ringworm—classmates'
heads shaved embarrassingly
round—or the multigraph
ink of impetigo. But they
were only a foreshadowing,
trial runs like measles
or chickenpox, little
preparations for the big
things the elders spoke
of with hushed awe: Rocky
Mountain Spotted Fever
was a good one with our parents
making us strip before bed
as they searched for the evil
ticks. If one was found
they had to make it back
out of your skin with
the lighted end of a cigarette.
(If you just pulled them off
the head stayed in and you
could die.) Any cough might
mean diphtheria or TB
and many spoke of the killer
flu after the war, shaking
their heads over the numbers
of the dead—many more
than died in the trenches.
In the muffled talk there
was a mix of terror

and fascination—almost
love—for these mysteries
circling in the swampy mist,
swirling us toward some wasting
away out there beyond the reach
of lamps. Sugar diabetes lurked
in every candy bar and if you
stayed out too late having
fun your heart might turn
rheumatic. And of course
there were the pursed lips
saying *cancer*, sotto voce—
and we felt its chewing teeth
out there with pincer claws
sharper than any knife.
But our parents reserved one
of the best just for us:
Polio would surely fester
and flower in our legs making
them stiff as FDR's if we
played too hard in the summer sun.

Tom Pete

He lived in the town,
a lonely old man I suppose,

but that was only the real Tom Pete.
My grandmother

invented the other one:
The fierce dirty prowler,

burning-eyed drinker at windows,
scratching finger on the screen.

She made him
a stringy-haired Hollywood Indian

with unbelievably silent moccasins.
He followed us home

from every movie,
Tonto's evil brother.

She said children went into his shack
and never came out—

he ate them like beans.
We were haunted speechless

by his great hunger for peeping,
his eyes able to draw

everything out through the window
like a blown egg,

like a seashell—
all your meat gone.

We understood nothing and everything.
He was always there whispering,

rattling the outhouse door,
crouching in the fruit cellar.

We believed nothing
and everything.

We never saw him
though we saw him everywhere.

Fret

From a thousand miles away
we could feel her worry—
it worked something like radio,

we decided, and seemed to hug
the invisible lines of latitude
to swarm around us on sunny days

and make us jumpy for no reason.
It brought clouds and gloom
and sleeplessness and made us

snap at each other like hungry dogs.
She had been our teacher—the way
she worried us back in the car

when we were halfway to a picnic
to see if she had put out her
Lucky Strike or left the iron on.

She was good at everything—fire, flood,
the natural disaster of a blowout
on the highway—but electricity

was her specialty, how all those
wires coiled in the walls could turn
white hot in the middle of the night

and burn us all to ashes in our beds.
Though she died quietly over
twenty years ago her worry still

travels far to nudge inside our walls
and we still lie awake, gritting our
teeth to keep those wires cool all night.

Pastoral

In those days blood seemed nearer
the surface and always ready
to flow—split lips, jackknife cuts,
scraped knees. I remember
my father coming late
from work—long after supper—
face streaked with sweat, looking
frighteningly old. And he seemed
covered with dust—little puffs
rose up when he shifted position
slumped on the spindly kitchen
chair, saying his shoulder hurt.
I had never heard him complain
then I saw a spreading spot of red
coming through his shirt. He was
too tired to eat but revived
with stories of run-ins with
the strawboss, a man called Hanks,
who came alive in the kitchen
like some fairy tale ogre and lost
every argument. Years later,
I understood how he hated that
work—the potato cellar a last
resort and dangerous for what
it said about a man—a job
for winos and drifters. That night
he winced as my mother pulled his
shirt free from his raw shoulder,
the glare of the bare bulb
seeming to hurt it all over again
like some degrading stigmata.
Those were hard days—the WPA
years away—and he refused
to sign on at Brown's mill
where they paid you with scrip
only good at Brown's store.

He wouldn't be one of Brown's
slaves, nursing along the last
sliver of independence left over
from the lost farm. The potato
cellar tested him with shame,
the burlap sacks keeping his
shoulder raw no matter how
it was bandaged. I remember
the rawness leaping into light
every night when my mother
peeled away the gauze, my
shoulder wincing every time.
And I remember him hissing
through his teeth and sighing
as the wound was bathed
and dressed. But he put up
with Hanks and his shoulder
all the way through the season.
By October the wound was healed.

Sunday Morning Walk

Boise was my first city,
a place I imagined
at the end of a perilous
road of gravel slippery
as marbles, a road
with ravines on both sides
like the one in *The Thief
of Bagdad*. But going there
offered only Horseshoe Bend's
handful of butterflies.

Later the schoolyard was
dangerous with strangers
and the building
had too many rooms,
too many echoes
in the halls. And there were
sidewalks everywhere.
Once a yard fetishist
yelled at me for daring
to step on his lawn.
I hadn't noticed but
after that I made
a point of crossing it
every chance I got,
wishing only that my
feet were bigger,
my footprints deeper.

Our apartment was small
and dark as a cave, much
smaller than the house
back home I knew
was gone for good.
There was little work
in Boise which made

my parents talk late
as our savings went quarter
after quarter into the gas
meter. But on Sundays
we took walks and the days
were good—late fall
with its bluster
and knife edge and longing
for snow. That Sunday was
windy, too, and clear as we
walked toward the treat
of a restaurant breakfast.
Leaves blew and the big trees
complained like old stairs.
There was no traffic.
Far off as in a movie
we heard the Extra shouted.
Only that word in and out
of the wind but as we
got closer the words
defined themselves one
by one and by the time
we bought our paper
the war had started.

WWII

Saving tinfoil and buying stamps
was our war. Even at eight
I thought wads of tinfoil
were a bit silly—as if they

could be thrown like silver
snowballs at Hitler. It seemed
too much like Aunt Jenny
with her miles of useless string.

But Roosevelt called for tin, too,
and we pitched in—secretly
longing for air raids—wheeling
a wagon full of dim battered pans

looking suspiciously like veterans
of the civil war. (Though one
woman, grinning with booze, gave us
a complete set shiny as chrome.

Later we heard she ran off
with a sailor.) Everyone wanted
to get into the act: "Lucky Strike
Green Has Gone To War!"

What we really wanted to do
was rescue Robert Preston from
Wake Island and tooling the wagon
around wasn't even like real work—

delivering papers you had to
get up early at least. The only
brief excitement came when
the Japanese navy sent some kind

of fire bombs on balloons into
the Coast Range. As I recall
one fireman burned his fingers
but they put the fire out quickly.

Needless to say we were never
lucky enough to get invaded.
So we were left with the dullness
of collecting—tinfoil, pots and pans

and rubber bands and the booklets
for defense stamps that always got
lost before they were half full.
The only casualty was the USS *Oregon,*

broken up for scrap though they
left her main mast planted beside
the Willamette. On a school outing
we all scratched our names in the metal.

Geography

In fourth grade we played Geography
every Tuesday, Mrs. Eustace
turning her blank globe slowly,
then stopping and poking her
long pointer at countries
seen only in outline.
Our hands shot up like
salutes—"Me, me, Mrs.
Eustace, me"—and ticked
names off with nine-year-old
aplomb: The Belgian Congo, Ceylon,
French Indo-China—
names now like dusty attic
souvenirs. But her pointer
never found some places—
Bataan where my young
uncle was taken prisoner,
Guadalcanal where Mr. Eustace
lost his leg. And we couldn't
know what other names that
blind globe was dreaming of:
Tarawa, Saipan, Okinawa,
Bastogne, Anzio, Monte Cassino.
Omaha Beach waited—in of all
places France!—for my best
friend's father to die
on D-Day. The globe kept
secret even stranger
lessons: Belsen, Treblinka,
Auschwitz, Hiroshima, Nagasaki.
How could we know that Mrs.
Eustace's key to her blank globe
with all the right answers
would be rewritten by history
until now it's mostly wrong—
the blush of the British Empire's

pink faded as the cheek of an
English rose—and would look like
one of those ancient maps that said,
Beyond Here There Be Monsters.

Carpentry

My father checks his rule, squints,
takes off his hat and swipes
a finger across his forehead
and then, finally sure, draws

the steady line of his broad
pencil on the two-by-four.
Slowly at first he pulls the saw
back and forth, then increases

the tempo, sawdust filtering down
like flour until the perfect cut
is made, the end piece plunking down,
the saw glinting free. Now comes

the brittle agony of wallboard, each
tiny finishing nail going in carefully
as a stitch, each section plumb
because of all the time he spent

staring at the level's gulping bubble.
He consults his metal rule again.
He measures corners over and over.
He sweats and swears them square.

Watching, at fourteen, I think it's
all some foolish pride, all this
painful care, all those hours
of searching for those elusive points

of stress. Now, I know his pride
went other ways—into the exact
tilt of his hat and the graceful
way a new suit fell or the savored

stories of his dance hall fights.
But I feel that stubborn thing
in him insist: Things must line up,
must run true, square is square,

plumb is plumb. It itches in
my fingers now as I balance
commas and vowels and tap in
the finishing nail of this period.

Blake in Idaho

My uncle and his
buddies fired their
.22s straight at rocks
loving the twanging
ricochets just like
cowboy movies.
They knew they were
immortal and at worst
would suffer only
flesh wounds any red
bandana could heal
fast. In fact, they
never hurt themselves
though once they ran
home without stopping,
afraid a slug had
bounced into a heifer
grazing too near
the rocks that twanged
the best. They believed
in the road of excess
and travelled it hard,
rapid firing as they
roamed the woods, loving
those ricochets the way
they loved to eat
and drink, getting sick
on every flavor. And what
difference did it make?
Two heard the real thing
in Korea and died;
one roared his '48
Merc toward the palace
of wisdom and found
a head-on collision.
The others were cut

down to size by life
like the rest of us,
working in the mill,
selling insurance,
learning far too well
the lessons of
the horses of instruction.

Slivers

My father's cousin
                      was death on slivers
and had that needle out
before you could hide your
                              toe or run.
She loved fishing in your
skin and it hurt
but she always worked
those minnow-slivers out
and the pain sighed out
with them.
             She had other talents too—
getting after warts
                      with whispered spells
or chasing fevers
                    with stumpwater potions.
She read tea leaves and palms,
even the moss on trees.
But she was tight-lipped,
we had to worm such news
out of her the way she fished
slivers out of us.
                    But if she was really
in the mood it was whole cloth
with all the embroidery—
our futures glowing with
adventure and big money, love—
though she always wangled
a few shadows in, a lifeline
that made her purse her lips,
tea leaves she
                washed down the drain
without a word.
                  When we thanked her
for digging out a sliver she sighed:

What else am I good for?
in a tone that made us
feel guilty for not hurting
ourselves often enough.
                              She always
stayed with us through August's
hottest days,
                    when slivers bloomed on
the bone-dry porch,
                              then moved on
as if carrying some muffled
sorrow in her black hatbox.
Growing older we puzzled
over why she moved around so much
and hoped for scandal
or, better, a childhood
sweetheart killed in action.
                              One Christmas
she showed up drunk and singing,
making us blink.
She swayed in the doorway and then
with perfect form, bowled
a frozen turkey across the floor,
yelling, How the hell
                              do you like that, Santa!
Nobody knew which way to look.
Then she was crying on her cousin's
shoulder and spent the night
in the back bedroom.
By morning she was gone.
During the next summer's
hottest days we fished our
own slivers out
and for every summer after that.

The Moment's Equation

The damp circles their bottles print
link arms across the table, circle
after faint circle, mysterious as magicians'
silver rings. But nothing pulls these rings

apart. They keep their own intimate
score, some written record of the hour
after work, the dusty revelations
of exhaustion cut by beer, resentment

and release fluttering like flies
with wet wings trying to fly. It's
the usual script of getting even with
the boss—my father sitting there, his

stories all "He says" and "I says,"
finally coming out on top of that yahoo
foreman. The others nod and drink.
But there is some cross-grained meaning

I reach for in the linked rings and the pattern
of cigarette butts in the ashtray.
It's a meaning like the wavy sweat stains
on hat bands and the worn spots on work pants,

it's in what is truly said by the burnished
silver corners of black lunch pails. Something
rubs and speaks there the way it speaks
in those hammer handles rubbed smooth

as glass and the business ends of shovels
brilliant as polished chrome.
These meanings stir below alibi and excuse,
written in codes lost below layers

of macadam spread steaming in summer heat,
pounded senseless again and again
by truck tires. My father tells his
stories, forcing words to win back

what was lost. His friends nod, squint,
and tell their stories too, slowly now
in this soothing gloom, air dark as ale.
They get even the only way they can,

linking their rings' zeros in this casual
parliament that endorses their days
and notarizes the moment's equation
with each round formally bought in turn,

smoke and beer-buzz thickening until every
boss who ever lived finally owns up that he's
a candyass sonofabitch and, finally redeemed, they
may now steer their own dark macadam home.

Fifteen

That spring there was always a piano
or its echo, two people playing
the two part "Heart and Soul."
I was pledging a secret society
with some Greek name I've forgotten—

me, a kid whose father was a day
laborer got a bid! We met in houses
like movie sets—carpets, dark
panelling, tiled bathrooms with
towels so soft and thick they felt

like fur. And there I was among
the sons of dentists and insurance
agents, sons who drove their own
cars, who had drawers full of cashmere
sweaters, who wore just the right

kind of saddle shoes. Over it all
the sound of "Heart and Soul,"
a sad beauty I floated on, nearly
breathless amid the layers of middle
class richness—they were sure

to catch on, I knew, and blackball
me to oblivion. But they didn't
and I stuck it out through the silly
fright of hell week until they
shook my hand as a brother.

For a while I was a member of that
world, swearing secrecy and bigotry,
swearing allegiance to a future
of car dealerships or podiatry,
all to the tune of "Heart and Soul"

like music in a Doris Day movie.

August Memories

Every bleached August I remember
the parched dust of pre-season,
sore knees wincing with wind sprints
and laps, grass drills without

any grass, the croaking voices
of coaches calling us chicken,
calling us sissies through those
weeks of pure dizzy August heat,

coaches yelling, come on girls,
let's see what you got! And we
ground on, heaving our guts out
after laps and sprints, spitting

cotton and bile, mouths drier
than the dusty field. Every day
the squad got smaller, the coaches
humiliating people away

with nutcracker drills—crowing
when a shrimp went against
a goon—calling them quitters,
gutless, no balls at all…

The rest of us stuck it out
through twice-a-days until
scrimmaging started and the croaking
volume turned up. Whatever it was

we never did it right. Hit
the two hole, stupid! Drive
your shoulder all the way through!
Don't try to hide out there,

we see you! Our little Devil's
Island went on seeming endless,
until we arrived at the first
pep rally—*Beck Beck he's our man*

if he can't do it Fowler can
Fowler Fowler he's our man...
which took us to the oasis
of the first game. Under the mystery

of the lights in our bright
new uniforms we clattered onto
the field while the rally girls
cheered and we became heroes

and loved every minute of it.

The Super 99 Drive-in Chronicle

We cut the lights before sneaking
through the low gate in back—
Carl slipping the latch, Jim giggling
dangerously, the rest of us hissing,
pipe down! The small danger
thrilled us, tickling our neck hairs—
that huge sound of the tires munching
across gravel over those endless
back rows, expecting a cop's
snooper, maybe even a siren.
We crawled like a mole to one
of the crowded lines and hooked up
a speaker, careful as safecrackers.
Mostly, we didn't care for the movie,
all anti-climax after that drumming
of sneaking-in fear made the skin
tight on our faces, and, bored, we left
at intermission looking for action
dragging Broadway's crowded
desolation past midnight's curfew.
The next year we parked on the road
behind the gate. The distant silent
faces on the screen meant nothing—
each of us was alone with a date,
trying like surgeons to learn how
to unhook a bra with two fingers,
aching to release those lovely
moons in the steely moonlight
while in the distance a mute Doris
Day flailed crazily as if protesting
what we tried to do, her honor at stake.
Nothing much happened though
until we bragged by the lockers
Monday mornings. Later, it got
serious. Going steady, we paid our way in,

raising everything to a higher level—
the speaker mumbling in our left ears
all through the movie we never watched.

Office Hours Ancestors and Drought

The clock cuts huge pie shapes
from what you want—a day
of rolling over and over in sweet grass...
And naturally enough, the mind wanders—
your ancestors spread out like a vast
delta behind you, all silt and the gritty
memory of bones.
You wander toward
the Midwest where they first
settled, eating sod and dreaming desserts
of dust bowl and drought.

About this summer's drought,
a woman on the radio says:
"It just keeps destroying the psychic
of the farmer." She got all dolled-up
for the interview, I bet, but where
is the farmer's psychic?
Would he have predicted
this terrible absence of rain?
Would it have done any good?
Maybe all he predicted
were higher food prices,
desperate to please, not daring
to tell why they would rise.

You table your emotions on the issue.
The clock keeps torturing you
with its oozing passage.
You vow never to look at it again.
And, like clock-work, you do so
immediately. And here your ancestors roll in
again, an army lost to the last trooper.
Only the first and second ranks
are at all clear, the others fade into fog
without faces or nametags.

But in your dreams—remember—
they rush forward with whispers like kisses,
telling you all their train whistle sorrows.

You long for the tall sweet grass,
the sea where you may give
broadsides of your dreams away,
where breezes caress you like a lover
or vice versa.

Bored with your dullness
and distraught because of the drought,
your ancestors pull up stakes, letting themselves
be sucked back across the Atlantic,
dodging ice floes and scurvy.
You volunteer to join them *or* Custer,
anything to get away from that clock.
Are its hands tied? Has it killed itself?

Deep in some freezer
the minutes of your life stand still,
inert as peas in a TV dinner.
You fumble for the foggy people of the past,
your fingers thick and cold,
dragged numb by this afternoon
as long as misery. And now
that we all need him, where oh where
is the farmer's psychic?

Field Burning

1.
Driving down the valley we see smoke rising
 thick, so thick it has the sculptured look
of something solid, like a kind of twisting
 clay rising, black richly marbled with gray.
For a change the wind is right and the smoke
 doesn't cross the highway, but we taste it
and feel the atmosphere off to one side,
 something dense and menacing as it
swirls up from the fields. They say
 such burning is good for the crops.
They say it's the only thing to do. And much
 noise is made about it here—many gray
committee faces worry their faces grayer still
 over the issue. But it is dramatic—
that smoke roiling as high as we
 can see, smothering the sun where it can.
Some signal fire to the stars, like something
 totally out of control that strangely isn't,
some desperate message that means nothing.
 But seeing it we know the American love
of cutting and burning—like the people up the street
 who just moved in and immediately cut that old
growth beside their driveway. Cut, then burned it.
 That side of their house is naked now
but they seem to like it. Much in us would like
 a continent of stumps, every forest
cut off at the knees. As we drive toward Corvallis
 I think of Marching Through Georgia,
scorched earth policies and other tags, and how
 that will to cut and burn burns deep
in us, that appetite for waste space gnaws
 within us with a tapeworm hunger
as if the first of us here needed to gouge
 and burn away his fear of wilderness

and how we carry on now with asphalt
     and concrete, wanting finally it seems
to close every breathing pore of the earth.

2.
As I drive I remember another field
     on fire. It was an August forty
years ago and the whole field bordering
     our grim street moved toward us
with that speed you never think a fire
     can have. And I remember my mother,
five months pregnant with my sister, fighting
     that fire, getting me and the panicky
neighbors organized with all the decisiveness
     generals are supposed to have but never do.
She whipped those hoses in place, got rugs wetted
     down and even gathered the street's
dull shovels together in case a trench was
     needed. The fire added an August
to that August and its roar rose like
     a semi climbing a grade as it poured
across that field toward us as if emptied
     from a thousand buckets. But with hoes
and wet rugs and some dented buckets
     of our own we turned it back
and watched it chew itself alive, eating its
     own hot thistles. We were astonished
with what we had done. Suddenly it was only
     a black field, all that threat of homelessness
gone up in smoke. I remember my mother's
     speed—how she ran from place to place,
smoothing or swearing panic into action.
     It was amazing to see. But I remember
my first embarrassment, too, as I watched her
     carry that belly into action while neighbor
women honked of miscarriage or worse,
     their eyes rolling in fear of fire.
She knew they had given up as they always

did on such streets, knew that without her
the whole numb street would burn, committing
   its own docile suicide, the men come home
to dinners of ash. Her soft voice grew fierce
   and the women's housecoats flew behind
them as they moved fast, following orders.
   Following orders, I worked too—all teenage
embarrassment gone—throwing hoses and drenching
   rugs, steering children toward the rusty
buckets. We won that one together, forcing
   the street to survive against its own mealy will.
Driving toward Corvallis I remember that
   August and chalk one up against fire—it
doesn't always win nor are all of us eaten
   with the need to cut and burn.
Some of us simply want a place to live
   and will turn fire inside out to keep it so.

III

Billie Holiday

On those last records her voice
sounds almost gone—
cracking, breaking—but hitting
notes wasn't the point.
She was after the bones of beauty
not the flesh. It was far
too late for anything else.
She sang what must happen,
what has, the death of gardenias,
the abyss that the abyss
falls into. It all scraped along
her phrases, extracting the horrible
meat hiding inside simple words,
in the space between each
word, between each note.
And she broke our hearts until
they could break no more,
then broke them one more time
just to make sure we got the point.
Art isn't on the surface,
not some decoration like frosting,
like a flower in your hair—
it's like a silk bag of pulverized
crystal, glinting, sharp,
able to cut in any direction.
Her voice filled every room
in our minds and showed how empty
each was, how desolate
the wind blowing through them
and yet with sticks and stones,
castoffs, garage sale losers
she furnished each one
with a shattered gritty beauty
just before she took it all away.

On Transcendence

In America we do too much,
adding stars when that
corner is already full, flailing the map
for more frontiers, making horizons
stretch like rubber bands.
We don't know when to stop.
We don't know how much is too much.
Elsewhere is always better,
some street that lifts us gently
off the hook, some dreamy banker
who cancels all our debts
with a holy ballpoint.
We throttle the present, we plow up
the only roads we have
and load our houses with ballast
for voyages they never take.
And whatever thing we hold is never
the right thing. Besides, the guy over there
has ours and we want it.
We want it bad because he's got it.
If he don't watch his damn step
we'll take it the hell away from him.
We don't like his looks anyway.

What's Out There Now

We pick the route that promises
small towns and long stretches
of those intervals we like—
misty clouds, firs touching
fingers over the highway,
vistas fading off into those
mysterious blue herringbones
printed on the mountains.
A town turns up parading
its single little street, its
genuine imitations, its
souvenir cheeseburgers. There's
the ennui of rusting tables
at the sidewalk café under
umbrellas for a brewer whose
taps ran dry twenty years ago.
(They say his wife ran off
with a slick drummer, mustache
neat as a bandaid.) The map
makes more promises—more taverns
of loneliness, more pictures
of Elvis painted on velvet,
more mills gone to dust, green
chains silent. But by now we've
had it with towns and seek
those breathing spaces in between.
But here we see the crewcut
of a clearcut, and here slopes
slide toward us without mystery,
hills saying No Vacancy
to bobcat or owl. We feel
the day dissolving and head
home fast, slashburns breathing
their fake mist down our necks.

Numbers Game

Lately the days practice a fierce
subtraction, giving us
handfuls of less than dust,
some anti-matter we call

our lives. What little we have
left—the sound of wind,
the lovely agony of winter trees—
ghost burglars steal from us.

We want to know how
this happens but no one
tells us. History just says:
The first time, tragedy,

the second time, farce.
But we need another brand
of answer beyond this
glibness. Some voice

out of the fire, some hoarse
whisper which says
getting by is so simple,
you just forgot the directions—

they're easy as a recipe
on a soup can. But by now
we think we've forgotten
how to follow directions.

We hear the wind but it
sounds false and the trees
say nothing but their
nakedness. We don't want

winter to go this deep
but it does, subtracting us
far below zero where everything
is less than empty, where

nothing will ever add up again.

Enough

It is enough that the arrows
fit exactly in the wounds
that they have made.

—Kafka

We think it's fine that X and Y
give us all the details

about eels or that someone else
makes us feel we should spend

our lives in cornfields
studying the penmanship of the grass.

And of course the musk ox
is important and the whale,

but don't we feel
guilty enough already?

It's all very fine to hear
of the migration of birds

and the turtle's deep religion,
but we have other problems.

Getting up is a problem,
sleeping is a problem,

having to speak when your mouth
is empty of a single syllable

is a problem:
and finding a way to smuggle your name

from one day to the next
is a real puzzle.

Our problems are near:
We can run aground

on a broken crankcase,
we can founder on a toothpick.

We live too close to the bone
where they say the meat is sweetest

but we know better.
If we get drunk too often

so what? What else can we do?
Our minds are jammed as attics.

We're filled with a dangerous pulse
and we have no time.

We must save the best for the wolf—
he counts on us—

and we're already too sensitive,
we need no training.

It's a good day when
you can blunt a nerve or two.

Most days we just want to lie down
and sink through the floor for good

with embarrassment and gloom.
But like fools we go on

looking for our names every day
on the edge of an abyss

like a grease trap.
Some nights the scraps of self-pity

are all we have left,
our inner life

below subsistence level.
We can't afford dreams,

we've given those rights away
to disc jockeys.

Our miracles are small—making ends meet,
curing the hand to mouth disease.

Bleached Grass

Once more I drive by
the bleached grass,
past the ditches
of lost hubcaps,
the sad shinbones
of the dry willows.
It is years ago.
A young man's aimless
restlessness sits
beside me. I try
to drive faster
than my thoughts
darting from sorrow
to sorrow, paging
through them for
the one good thing
slipped between
each wincing pain.
The grit of sleeplessness
under my eyelids,
I listen to the tires
sigh, breathe in
the dusty nothingness
of dead weeds,
read the scrawl
of rusted wire
holding the exhausted
fence posts up.
And behind it all
I hear the babytalk
of death, the crooning
of the abyss. I croon
back with a country
music whine, thistles
caught in my throat.
The road travels

farther to the past,
crawls back to
gravel and then dirt,
then only wagon ruts
losing their way
in high grass—wilderness
without adding its
dark codicil to
the wilderness within.

Families Returning

It is after dark and the small
       cars purr to stops, headlights
              lowered demurely. The wicker
evening has been used up and summer
       wades away toward September.

Fathers carry in the tangled sleeping
       loaves of the smallest children.
              The older ones speak too loudly
because of the sudden strangeness of their
       dark houses and this moment

in their lives, a moment they may
       remember years from now
              when everything has changed
forever. But the parents hush them
       and so they caper silently

with frisbees and hampers, choking back
       giggles as streetlight sifts down
              a kind of mysterious dust,
an evanescence caught in their eyelashes.
       At the doors locks fumble with

keys as fathers shift babies, trying
       hard not to spill a single
              drop of their sleep.
Mothers find the anemones of light switches
       and the houses blaze their emptiness.

After the babies are lowered delicately
       into their cribs, the others
              gather in their kitchens,
feeling parched in the locked-in air.
       They throw windows open

and have final solemn drinks
before wading slowly toward
their alien September beds,
blinking back the dusty brilliance
caught in their eyelashes.

Industrial Relations

That summer we worked in boxcars
with huge forks to scoop cans on an
endless belt so the world could have
more canned peaches than it needed.

Eight hours a day in the hundred
degree heat, our only air from
the open door, with those ten-tined
forks we scooped and placed, scooped and placed—

row on row of shining zeros—
a ten minute break every two
hours. For rest and fun every so
often we jammed a can sideways

and laughed as the cans shot up like
rockets and they shut the line down
for repairs. We grinned to ourselves
when the hard-hatted engineers

in white shirts and neckties came out—
sliderules slung on their hips like guns,
infinities of pens in their
pockets like ammo—and scratched their

heads over another breakdown.
They fiddled with their clipboards, tugged
at the belts with fussy fingers
and then, tentatively, started

the line again and we were back
at it, lifting those forks until
quitting time or until we jammed
another can sideways starting

the ritual all over again.
All summer long the spic and span
engineers never figured out
why the breakdowns occurred and we

stopped the line any time we pleased.

Cannon Beach Meditation

I
For years local tides measured
our lives, the sea watching
and sighing, muttering her ironic
footnotes, scattering broken
sand dollars on the beach.
We called it small change—
those shells pounded to nickels
and dimes by the surf, chickenfeed
we scorned.

II
       We kept at it though
and tonight I hold this nearly
perfect one, the last dollar
left over from those lost days.
I trace the flower it drew
on itself—almost a fleur-de-lis,
almost a snowflake. Turned around
it's the drooping leaves
of a dying plant, flipping it—
which is heads? Tails?—my finger
travels tiny arroyos. They wriggle
in soft light like the lines
in our hands telling the same
senseless stories.

III
       That lost life
stalks near me now, a life
that goes on and on like the sea.
I feel its nearness, almost smell
it in the October air—no two
leaves the same color and the sky

flying away from my reach like
everyone's lost dreams. Its long
narrow spirit never sinks and I
hear it, always walking away toward
winter, echoing.

IV
          The shell's notched
edge ratchets me back to those days
we became tycoons, the Pacific
depositing dollar after perfect dollar
into our account. I squeeze this one,
pressing for the surf's beat,
my breathing and the sea's muttering
joined in song. Snapshots of us
catch between each breath, catch
then let go, drifting beyond memory
before another snags, lodges briefly,
then takes its turn toward oblivion.
We scoured the high tide line, dashing
into the watery ice—another one!
Another one!

V
          Our dreams came true
all week, paying us off for the years
of penny-ante work we'd done culling
the dimes and pennies. I stretch
out toward those days but touch only
this shell, old and dry but still
holding a few grains of sand—like
the stubborn grains we couldn't wash off
and carried to breakfast like secret
condiments, but finally knowing we
were singled out, history's darlings
at last!

VI
        In October sleep our streets
widen and the city migrates far—
even our rooms grow, becoming parks
and playing fields, the third floor
an Everest away. Every surface stretches
thin as onion skin and lets me
hear you in your old rooms—turning
in bed, speaking your sleep language.
I almost climb the stairs to welcome
you back. But all I can do is speak
to you here and recall how we never
made such a killing again. We had
to prorate that one great haul over
all the other flat-broke summers.
And today I found only this one,
the others frittered away
by spendthrift attic shadows, I guess.
But I use this one to try to
buy back those days at cost.

VII
                                I feel
the Coast Range cringe, leaning east.
Winter sends its message along
the surface, letting the dew change
to ice on cue, putting an end
to summer's propaganda, saying I'll
be in charge soon. Then I'm paged
back to June days and the cottage
they took away in one of America's
silly games of hide and seek, taking
with it so many of our hours
of surf dreaming into our sleep,
erasing every view from those windows,
burying the calendar of those
seasons.

VIII

      Holding back winter with
one hand, I look hard for our
rich summer, moving past icy tides
and fog, digging up one and then
another, resurrecting sand castles,
letting thoughts drift out with boat
lights strung along the horizon's
dark wire. I walk all our old paths.
I fly with our AWOL kites. I want
to find each mystery footprint
and those summers locked in the closets
of the lost cottage. I grip the dollar.
I let it slow me down. I turn it
like a dial, checking each summer back
into those rooms one by one, making
them sign the register. It all seems so near now—
surf and sound, sand—and I turn the dial
one more time and we're scouring those
icy tides again—Another one! Another one!

Reunion on the Weekend of the Fourth

With only three days free
I drive straight through tonight,
tasting sagebrush,
                          pushing hard
all the way to the rodeo
grounds on the edge of town.
Memories collect there,
ghosts filling the bleachers,
recalling how blond those
rails used to be.
                          In town
Bob and Ruth sway in time
to jukebox cries of divorce
and flaming highway
wrecks
             whining from the bar.
We pass each other
our ages like schoolroom
notes when we shake hands—
Ruth's hair gray, the circles
of three marriages
                          under her eyes.
Bob holds his Air Force
pension like a missal—
he's still thin but stooped
with the espionage
of Agent Orange.
                          I show what
I've become.
                   They nod, making
no judgment.
                   Still shy we swap
pictures of our kids
like passports to middle age
then go in the bar, grabbing
a dim table in the corner.

We all order drinks
fancier than we want,
not as hard as we need
but they help,
                    oiling our tongues
toward memory's common
ground—the swamp, the lake,
sledding downhill
                    in the dark,
all the times we fought,
their cheap shots
                    and mine.
They recall the day
                    I straddled
their hill shying rocks just
close enough to make
them jump
                    until their old man
came out and swore me
home
        and how my mother swore
him red-faced back
up the hill.
                    Here we bury
our parents once again,
giving no details.
                    Fancy drinks
grab hold and we talk
icehouse and tadpoles,
pumping stories into legends
until they slowly lose air
and we recall our lives
starting out
                    on the straight road
to Boise until they hit
Horseshoe Bend,
                    how they never
were the same again.
                    By now

the air is thick
with the molasses sadness
of country songs.
We hum along
                    filtering out
our private truths from coyote
howls, their heavy-handed
sorrows mixing with our own.
As usual we've missed
the fireworks
                    and near closing
time exchange addresses
and profound promises
to keep in touch
                    then sit back
watching our addresses blur,
zip codes and street names
mingling and fading
on wet bar napkins
                    as if wanting
to forget themselves.
                    We look
at them and laugh, each
of us having learned
just how much
profound promises are worth.

The Richard Snyder Publication Series

This book is the seventh book in a series honoring the memory of Richard Snyder (1925-1986), poet, fiction writer, playwright and longtime professor of English at Ashland University. Snyder served for fifteen years as English Department chair, and was co-founder (in 1969) and co-editor of The Ashland Poetry Press, an adjunct of the university. He was also co-founder of the Creative Writing major at the school, one of the first on the undergraduate level in the country. In selecting the manuscript for this book, the editors kept in mind Snyder's tenacious dedication to craftsmanship and thematic integrity.

Snyder Award Winners:
1997: Wendy Battin for *Little Apocalypse*
1998: David Ray for *Demons in the Diner*
1999: Philip Brady for *Weal*
2000: Jan Lee Ande for *Instructions for Walking on Water*
2001: Corrinne Clegg Hales for *Separate Escapes*
2002: Carol Barrett for *Calling in the Bones*
2003: Vern Rutsala for *The Moment's Equation*